SOME OTHER MORNING

D0555700

SOME OTHER MORNING

POEMS BY JEREMY DRISCOLL

STORY LINE PRESS

1992

© 1992 by Jeremy Driscoll

First American Printing

All rights reserved. No part of this book may be reproduced in any form or by any electronic or mechanical means including information storage and retrieval systems without permission in writing from the publisher, except by a reviewer.

This publication was made possible thanks in part to the generous support of the Nicholas Roerich Museum, the Andrew W. Mellon Foundation, and our individual contributors.

ISBN: 0-934257-66-3

Book design by Lysa McDowell

Cover illustration by Claude Lane, O.S.B.

Published by Story Line Press, Inc.

Three Oaks Farm in Brownsville, OR 97327

TABLE OF CONTENTS

POEMS FROM SOME MORNING (1980)

POEMS FROM THE NIGHT OF ST. JOHN (1989)

*For good friends in many parts of the world
whom I met during my years of study
in Rome, 1980-1990.*

ANY DAY, ANY NIGHT

AN INTRODUCTION BY WILLIAM STAFFORD

Suppose whole generations could by degrees lose their vision, could harden themselves and gradually adjust to what they saw as a diminishing role for openness and adventure....

Someone—Wittgenstein?—speculated about how philosopher-prisoners can adjust to their cell, where they hammer away at the walls and rattle the window bars; but if they would just turn around, the door is open.

The poems in this book offer that liberating turn again and again. For the way of the spirit, the world is as open and promising as it ever was. And life—even in our time— no matter how restricted or astray, abounds in choices. A kind of April freshness awaits the inquiring spirit.

This readiness for the redeeming turn lives throughout these pages, where the language flows easily, talk-adaptable and neighborly, conducting the reader as a friend. Jeremy Driscoll's poems do not so much oppose the negative as they ignore it, flowing around, finding what always was there waiting.

How could we have plodded so long, and bent our thoughts and feelings downward, and assumed that our lives need be enslaved by fashions in intellect that shadow The hours? Can it be that the world we have allowed to turn stony and dark around us can be illuminated with so quiet a touch as these poems provide? In one poem, about Easter, the author simply remarks, "This is the day the Lord has made." This manner of seeing, or this flash of recognition, is typical of Father Jeremy's prevailing attitude, the friendly sharing of a calm assumption. "We are accompanied / in what we do," he says, and readers are reminded of the ways of a time many have thought to be lost. Those ways come lightly along in these poems.

Two earlier books by Father Jeremy, *Some Morning* and *The Night of St. John*, combine here with new works to make *Some Other Morning* a fulfillment for earlier readers and a discovery for new ones. The kind of discovery may be hinted at in words that helped introduce that earlier work: "The ambition of these poems is for something beyond literature. Their way of proceeding is to invite us into new experiences of 'mighty moments' that come 'in a great flash of peace.'"

EPIGRAPH
THE VALUE OF A BIRD

Bird, Bird,
Bird, bring me.
I'd come with you back to the sea.

You can give me
the ways through the sky.

I'll have bright wings beating,
    slapping at salty air,

new cares and peace.

I YIELD TO TIME

I am began and a start
and then at length and at last—this face.
        But certainly not exactly this face for ever.

No, this one only until now
and this one only as
        on the way from somewhere
        and only as elsewhere half already gone.

And as lonely as that too.
As lonely as only a face for awhile.

        I am only a face for awhile.

Same Race, hello and ah (!)
 fleshed grace
 in your flushed cheek
 raised high   by
 the smile.

Same Race, Good Day to you
  and a sort of shock I feel
  that these faces—yours and mine—
  refract the fact
  of a same species here.
  Yet so unlike you: *me.*
        And we:
  so unlike (there are) billions of others
  and have been.

Same Race, I am full blushed
  when beauty wins again within the space
  —and so distinctively—
  within the rules
        of a nose
        mouth
        and eyes.
I am *unmasked* by your *mask*
  and so say:

Tame Face, look here toward me
   where I stand anxiously and truthfully.
   My mask fallen, what's under would tell

Wonder—half worshipful of you
Awe—fully adoring the Maker of you
Hope—that my thoughts similarly invade the mind of you.

Face! Threshold to the shrine called
   Thou, O You, The Other.

Thou   art   an   art.
You   are   yours.
O Other,   there   is   not   another.

Art thou art, in that beauty reigns and tells.
Yours you are, in that I see you self-possessed.
Not another, in that you differ even from your mother.

What brings it on, the form and glow?
One feels a serious radiance in the glance you throw.
I just know you know you know.

No, there is no other.
        In this you are like God.
Yes and you look to me and say, "Thou, O You."
        Likewise like God in this.

                (Bliss, O Bliss!
                You make me then, you make me to be.
                You beget and I am begot
                 and in this we are strongly a we.)

And when after this kiss we look beyond and say, "Others!
Others!"
Beyond ourselves being,
in this (bliss!) being,
we are like God.

Tact! (as touching) when I greet the visitors come.
Tact! For well worthy they
and come a long way

so the proper touch might give them
             much and much refreshment.

But Tact! Proper touch means
             not too much to touch.
And so I shall savour their coming and their coming in,
and their coming in and their being in
             can be easy and slow
and I will touch a little welcome
and lay my lips lightly on.

I touch a clean cloth to the table now,
across the table I lay it down.
I light a lamp there, I touch a flame on.
The bath I'll show and their rooms,
             and I'll let them be,
             let them be to be with me

and slow-ly
across my threshold come
             they will be
touched by all they see,

and from within my home
the whole world will be intact
as they are shown

    that in me
    delight
    overflows
    (too much?)
    overflows
    at their coming.

A voice in me said:
>I am still here.
>I am still clear.
And I needed that reminding sound,
for years are moving on in me.

I know what brought it up
I know exactly when it spoke

>when an apple held in my hand under the oaks
>crunched clean in my mouth and sprayed slight the sun
>inside me,
>the sun falling all around through the trees,
>grasses underneath a screaming flashing green,
>all like happened once when I must have been seven

>yes and the little grove's road climbing steep and
>bending easy,
>a road and a bend like when I first ever noticed
>>that a road curved and climbing
>>is a brilliant way to go.

So I climb a road again
and up over the top
the bend sets me loose in the sky
and there all bright I see

my face as a boy
my life as a boy
I hear my voice as a boy
and it says

You are still me.
You still love the autumn woods.
Good how you still run,
good how you walk and how you move.
Good the way you laugh.
Go on going.
I am still here.
I am still clear.

Down easy do I lie under birches and
up through lacy branches and yellowing leaves
I peer past an autumn and into a winter long gone,
     —yes, a winter, somehow a winter—
seen above the trees in the cool day sky.

> *The forest still slept that day after noon under a blanket of snow,*
> *yet it was willing to wake if some energy gave cause.*
> *Then someone cried, "Poets and boys to the woods!"*

> *Beautiful and swift we were, we boys.*
> *We moved with grace.*
> *We could climb a hill quickly or run it down.*
> *We were light and fast in talk and thought.*

> *So we hit that wood fast*
> *and we shook it loose tree by tree*
> *branch by branch we pulled that blanket down.*
> *Thumpingly it came down*
> *till at last at least a little our words could echo*
> *and the forest hear our cry:*

> *"Alive.   Alive.   Alive.   It's winter, boys!*
> *It's beautiful.   And we're alive."*

Why I see that moment flashing now,
I cannot say.
Is it that I hear that glad cry sounding in me again today,
years and seasons later?
Yes, these birches wave the same lines over me now:

Alive.   Alive.   Alive.   It's autumn.
It's beautiful.   And I'm alive.

I can exactly give you *this moment*
and then we can have it together
      if you will please bend your ear way over
      toward these words I am putting down.

This moment is me wondering why I always try
to get some sentences on a page
      every time some good thing hits me when I'm alone.

Why not just be here
by myself and by myself
stand amazed at, say, this night's stars pouring
      pins of light out over me
and stand pleased at how cool this darksome hour
and them, the stars, responsible, it seems,
      for even the night's slight winds.

Other times move in me like this one moves now. Many times.
      Birds in flight. Faces in different lights.
      Trees in certain tall relations to each other.
But why a poem? I will be alone. Something
strikes and then I'll try for the poem.

Alone I keep finding a meaning for us all, I think.
So what I do is
      I come toward you with a poem and ask,
      "Is this it? Would this be
      a way to say it? Help me."

Reader, whoever you are, hello!
I give you *this moment*

which is me wondering why I give it
and which is you
bending your ear over toward words
and receiving it.

This boy was keen.
In body, tending toward lean.
This has to do with what was seen
in-between.

This boy had insight.
In this he was right.
It made him strong, it was his might.
Sight.

He saw   everywhere   he saw Love.
In a dog, in a dove.
Below and above.

And always he called Thanks
for each of Love's wide pranks:
for the fire in the flesh
raised high in angels' ranks.

AQUINAS PERCHED
(In Viterbo Perched)

Seven hundred and more years ago—

    so that the people could have
    the very sky above them
    when the Preachers preached

an ambo was fixed
    outside
high up along the wall of the church

where a fat and holy man could climb and cry
    "Repent!"
and then the message would not sting so strong

because all the birds and the sun on the stones of the square
(so beautiful, so light, so fair)
would be there offering their own obedience to nature's ways
and add their tones to the preacher's pleas.

The trees could bend to the Gospel's breeze
and everything everywhere invite everyone
    to bend toward Grace
    to be bathed in Grace
    to fly upward toward Grace.

Winter's crisp clear cold snaps the mountains
    and the lake below
into sharp
      precise
           relief,

Relieved at last from not being seen,
from not being loved.

Yes, now the morning's chilly blue
has made my seeing new.
I am climbing.
I see everything.
And I love it.

My visible breath
is an invisible angel's trace
dangled before my face

    and climbing

I become friends with this angel,
who carries a scroll he wants unrolled,
who lightly goes all round me
and I see his opening band:

this world uncurled—
mountains,
a bright blue freezing sky
a lake low below lying
    exactly still,
      exactly a mirror.

And though this lake I love lies far away,
I can read the scroll it gives back.

Wisdom, it says.
Mercy, it reads.
All this for you, I see it say.

The rocky walls are streaming
with graces from your faces, O Christ.
Everywhere a falls,
everywhere a racing stream.

And now I think we are climbing up round to the places
where I might see these faces and but a few
of your thousand eyes,

but, no, I see first your sturdy mountain neck from behind,
shaking and make shimmer that waterfall hair you have.
And then glancing light from your eye the sun
(unveiled from behind a cloud)
crashes through everything I see
and burns a joy and fear in me,

and now I am praying afraid that I am a long time unready
to look you in the eye and receive from you
the full power of the mercy which comes
everywhere flowing down these mountains.

"A thousand eyes," I think.
"And could I but bear a single one?"

When suddenly the train is in a tunnel.
All turns black and my face
is reflected back from the window where
I watched for you.

Then I hear you say
—your voice the train's tunnel roar—
"There! Two eyes. And you bear them rather fine."

Out of the tunnel, the voice and the face are gone,
and I see now you've put on trees for jewels
and are dancing with them for me
straight up into the sky.

I shall ride on like this.
I shall await your every sign.
I shall bend my ear to your every roar.

When they put me down here
—I knew they had to; I was not angry—
I expected only the dark and the damp cold
and long boring years of hoping for the resurrection.

Imagine my surprise, then, when
not ten minutes after they had cried their last and gone
I sensed some. . .
    some breathing coming toward me
    through the ground.

It was distant, very distant,
but it was growing stronger,
and it was definitely coming my way.
What was it?

I wondered much and was worried.
Yet as it drew closer, fears faded some
and gave way to—I can only call it—
    my curiosity;
for as I say, I had expected nothing
to hold my interest here.

As the breathing drew closer,
I slowly discerned that it was
    the breathing of a song
and growing closer still, I could say
    the song of a throng,
and closer still, at last the words:

"Sanctus. Sanctus. Sanctus,"
they cried,

and I perceived this the song of those who had died
and now praised the Lamb
as Lord of heavenly armies.

This song was coming to stir and roll me over
    in my grave,
the which it managed
    before too long to do.

Then famous people came my way
and other saints from epoches and struggles
I never knew. Wraiths all,
they came round my grave
and breathed their song through my lowly corpse.

Bright Light saw I then
and struggled upward in my spirit
to see clear again. I saw:

A soft green mixed with faint rose
in the robes of a tenors' chorus,
and as their song passed through my being
a kind of recognition quivered
    in both them and me:
    Lovers of Christ. Brothers of Christ.
    Robed in colorly glory.

Toward my toes, white robes marked a virgins' chorus,
a crowd mixed with mothers and martyrs,
    both clothed by red.

Blue was there too on many whom I saw,
Blue and every color of an autumn.
Not one there was
    unmagnificent
    undazzling,
No one unshining.

All, in fact, was now a shining and a sound
moving through my plot of ground.
And I was being blended to their Light
and so sang with them,

   "O Might. Might. Might-y Lord!
   How vast, how glad this savéd hoard!
   How breathe we twice,
   unsnared from vice?
   O Might. Might. Might-y Lord!"

Straining further these new senses mine,
I tried to gaze where these veterans stared.
What cared I more that I was dead?
I turned with these toward Christ our Head
and sang with them the gladsome song:

   Sanctus. Sanctus. Sanctus.
   Dominus Deus Sabbaoth.

O gentle friends among the living still,
you yet but half alive,
pass by this plot with care.
"A graveyard is a spooky spot," you'll say;
but the ground a different story would to you now tell.

Destined to be on the Last Day
the place of a most amazed upstanding,
it is already stirring.
It is already moved.
It is already singing.

The desperate dog is baying long,
for his farm is empty of folk tonight.
It's Saturday, and everyone's gone to town
      dancing.

But I hear you, Booby-Pup,
    (two fields away and across the road)
and I understand how you feel.
I'm alone tonight too.

Your voice feels good, doesn't it?
You hear yourself, you say yourself,
you throw yourself way up high in the wind
and you don't think about it too real directly,
      but you kind of wonder, don't you,
      if something out there might not hear you
      and come.

Well, I'm coming in my own way.
Oh, I'll stay here where I am alright,
but I'm extending the human mind to you.
It comes over there right beside you where you're howling
and it wraps this good intention
around your cocked back throat
and its trajectory of sound:

Easy. Easy. Easy.
It's not so bad to spend a night alone.
You've got your health. You've got your bones.
You're strong. You'll be running free again tomorrow.
Easy, Booby-Pup.
I love you. You're not alone.

Some time passes, and
now it's grown quiet again.
Is the dance over so early?
Or maybe the desperate dog felt me come.
Anyway, something through the silence is now reaching me
and saying:

Easy. It's not so bad to spend a night alone.

PROBABLY ONLY INWARDLY SEEN
BUT MAYBE ALSO OUTWARDLY
(for my friends in Graz)

From one same dream summoned,
    we are taken up
    in dance
    in the predawn
    sky

And with some *Power* under our feet
we move agile, we are swift
along roofs steep and long.

The children hear us first. And they stir.
Then shortly after, the old; and they stir.
Later, lovers wrapped together unfold
    and smile toward each other, rested.

The dance is boy-girl-boy
    soft hand, rough hand, soft,
and we are swirling circles, marking rings of something
    up over our town
and in spinning the times our feet touch down
    tapping roofs in brief landings
    and then they're up (!) again, the feet,
    pointedly
    to the sky.

40   When a church's clock strikes seven,
it shakes its snow some
and now a good day is opening all over the town.
People (awakened by us without knowing)
are stirring and shaking and are on their way.

I wake to the seven strokes and do not remember this dream until
        sipping coffee
I think about what I'll do today, and then

        I see these faces of my friends
        so glad and fresh in the sky
        and I wonder,
        Was that a dream?
        Or did we just now really do that?

            And if only a dream, how is it then so
            that the whole town this morning
            is waking good.
            Rested. Joyful. And good.
            With rings of something
            up over us in the air.

The little city on the mountain is a jewel
      (one blue jewel)
The valley all around below it is a jewel
      (one green jewel)
and here we are, you and I,
watching the bright gem sun
go down slowly on the jewels.

My arms are around you and
your words float up slowly round my ears,
but the sunset breeze carries them cooly past
and though I hear you, I am not listening,
for I think:

      Surely what you say is that,
      we are those olive trees, green and gray
      and now gold in the sun,
      swaying and hugging the slope of the town.

      Or surely what you say is that,
      our hearts are dancing on this town's roofs.
      Red the roofs, but spanking red
      when the sun goes down.

      You must be saying,
      the church bells ringing
      are bringing angels down around us

and tonight—Easter Tuesday—
wild, sweet risen Christ
stalks the streets of this town.

Two boys kick their ball till the sun is gone.
Two birds fly the sky till the sun is gone.
Two friends talk till the sun is gone.

Now I tell the glory of the valley.
I tell it green and true
    beneath sky white and blue
and I tell from tall mountain.

I say (first I say):
    Down! Beyond and Down!
And what flatness there is
by the mountain's edge
and how it goes on,
    how it does go on,
poised and placed and stretched and held,
going gladder and more green.

Crops. Quite a lot. Quite a lot of crops.
    And each one
creeping out at different pace
(and so shade)
        of green.

And in the out there far and down distance,
    plowed and proud lands
    grieve the blade's solid slice
    and sulk in brown insistence
            that the deed be seen
            before they'll spring green

and there is so much more to say
so much more for the fields in their place
to say.
And so forth.

Yes, Forth!
"Forth," I say with and to the fields.
Forthwith.
Forth more the green
and all things seen.
And forth, in-seeing eye mine.
Further forth and be

more inwardly
in va-alley

for more clear-ly
telling
glo-ry.

Valley and Glory.
And bright clouds on the day's blue sky.

"Set a boy's bright brown eyes by a lake,"
said the painter to himself
and then put down first *blue*
for the lake.

Evening came and morning followed,
Painting's first day.

"And perhaps some trees in a breeze,
surrounding the lake, framing it," he thought.
So he put down *green*,
long tall swipes of green,
he made them wave and they were trees.

Evening came and morning followed,
Painting's second day.

"Under the trees some wild flowers
and maybe a few bugs on the bark or something."
Then many *colors* flew,
and the flowers were sweet to smell
and the bugs went crawling.

Evening came and morning followed,
Painting's third day.

"Now the boy," said the painter. "How shall I do this boy?"
And he worked hard, and he was never satisfied.
Days passed, and he painted on and he would try to get the legs

        so they were running
        and finally they were running
and then he struggled for the arms, he wanted them loose and light,
he wanted the boy running and his arms
        twisting upward
        from joy,
        for the lake
        made the boy glad,
        always glad.

Finally he tried the eyes, and on the eighth day he got the eyes.
He put down *brown* by the blue
and at last made the brown so somehow bright
that the whole lake—still and deep—stood in those eyes.
They had the movement of the swaying trees.
They were eyes like flowers.

And so now the painting was done,
and he saw that it was good.

He blows just a little to dry the eyes and face when
What this!
The child leaps lithesome from his plane
and stands dimensioned in the room.
The child bows low,
        kisses his Maker,
           looks around,
                sees color everywhere,

and then writes long all the lines of this poem.

On a mid-September morning Weather whispers a new song:

> *Cooler nights now, cooler nights from now on.*
> *Winds that'll send birds south again.*
> *Frost before long. Before long the frost*
> *and fog that'll crawl beside the rivers.*

And on this same morning I see:

> Two birds in circling flight.
> (Not-going-south-yet Birds, these.)
> Two gently circling birds
> with wings wide against the brightening vault.
> And these birds are trailed each in flight
> —this is my vision—
> by it is, it seems,

> > *some invisible twine*
> > *which traces and ties*
> > *a lacy web in the skies,*

> weaving a pattern impossible ever hoped unstrung.

This is the new season cinched into the skies.
Weather twisted her corner in the night
and now she cannot go back.

And who would want her to!
I take my lesson from these birds who sew
   Time's forward flowing to the sky,
and I taste from their swirling flight
   hope at Wisdom's promise
   in a season's change.

These two birds will go.
Leaves will shout, "Color!" and then, "Color, go soft,"
and then later they'll fall.
Eventually the snowbirds will come
to bind Winter to the sky.

All the while I will be here watching,
watching and going on with my life.
And I shall breathe in easy each day
   Wisdom's plan
   for me and my planet,
breathe it in from the air which carries Weather and Seasons along,
   for this is Time carried so.

Then when at length my day comes,
I shall (I hope) be ready—even willing—
to let some bird sew my finish in the sky:

   a last season passed,
   a last day,
   a last breath of air from some season's day,
   gratefully drawn in
   and then gracefully traced by a bird in the sky.

The flight of a dove
with the intention
of landing and
later
leaving where she
lands.

She leans back
softly
going forward
winging backwards so to land
not down here
but above in the top of a tree

on a top so
new
so new this spring
that it doesn't know
how
it doesn't until she the dove
lets up a little on the bending,
wings
stopping now
with the bending and the balance
just right.

The tree, a new lesson learned.
The rested dove moving on.

As we were digging
we knew that it was work
and we wondered
how heavy is the whole planet
is it dark if there is no space
or air
is a rock dark inside
was it dark in the rock before it split.

As we were digging
it was to be doing everything now
not to be
    on
the earth with nothing but space
between my hips and the moon
between
me and Mercury

it was to be
    in
    the earth up to our
    waists
    and digging

was to be doing everything
at once
    to be dying
    to be working
    to be making
    to be moving the earth
       barely
and inside of it
       barely
but enough.

We bring some light into the earth
and some air.
We shift a little somewhat
the weight of the
    planet.

SEAL

I wonder where
the seal is now
who twenty years ago
looked at me.

Did she swim north from here?
How have her days been,
the graceful twisting of
her body in a
green sea?

O swimmer, I would
thank you now for
your eyes so suddenly
cast when in our looking
we shared a
knowing before a
squirming away
that said,
"Remember. Now
you know."

I have not forgotten
what your eyes in the ocean
showed me:
We are accompanied

in what we do. Our days
look at us, and
they grow to be familiar days.
Recognized.

You teased me, seal,
to pull away
so quickly, inviting me
so young toward a
lifetime game of
suddenly seeing eyes.

For gratitude or
out of reverence, I
wish I could make
a sign toward you. If
you are dead, to bury
you perhaps. Or do
your children swim these
seas? To do for them
a favor once. I
am hoping that you
survived the hunts.

I have danced through days
and laughed with them.
I could swim my dance
in the sea. If I
could find you, seal, to

look again, I'd make my eyes
be the first to
duck and leave you
teased and knowing
that I have
remembered it.
I did not forget.

Can you
recall the
leaves, when in
October
we rushed past
them going
home from our
school,
and, O my sister, the
dark would
fall, for it had
become the night
and in bed in
our house the
birch was
my voice against
your window and
yours against mine
laying up with
the wind its
stringy voice
against the pane.

And if I
slept, the other
side of the wall,
the tree was

a ghost as
you lay awake
in the night
listening
and growing old.

Other children play
and sleep in our same
home. Is the
tree a ghost
for them. And do
the leaves
crack the
same messages
in the sad
cozy days of
the fall.

Now as you sleep
in your far
away place
and as you
wake, we
are the same
race, you and I,
O my sister.
The night
comes down differently
now and a

ghost that you
do not know.
But tread him
down. Each
stirring against
your window in
the night
is still the voice
of your brother,
just the
other side of
the wall. Still
awake. Not
sleeping yet.

SEA GULLS

For a long time blowing
sea gulls wait against being
pushed by an old north wind.

It comes thick and late from the north
blowing down hard now.
Cold.

The whole sky with sea gulls
facing to the wind. They
have found the pocket and
they've come in together
to play in the wind:
weight down
dipping and shooting—
and shooting
shooting up on it
facing still
waiting here
steady above this shore
this far up and
unpushed south
by the hard north wind.

They are the firm specks of white,
heirs of an old tradition with centuries of this.
Why do they wait
facing
except but that they can.

And it is their custom.

Everything that's along the water has a reflection.

I like when I can go down along the lake about four
and maybe find you there,
maybe not.
I like going with the hope,
and waiting.
Everything is more by one again.
The water is going to reflect the sky
and it goes right over the trees.

Every tree pokes the water.
And maybe you are there among the trees somewhere.
Maybe you might poke the water and I would see.

I want to stop and feel the damp shade.
I want to stop and hold a feeling just
as still as the water holds the trees.
I want to stop and wait for you
and try, if I see,
to hold you in my looking just as
still as the feeling
and the water holding the trees.

EASTER VIGIL

The rain is as soft
as a tomb cracking.

With the moon in the west,
around the fire we wait
for the sun.

And against the night
comes the day. Against
the night comes our song
and our brave gathering,
our walking, our circling,
and our standing. We throw
water and fire and smoke
into the night, and
our eating is against the night.

There is the standing up into the air
of all things renewed.
There is the going up into the sky
of the sun.
There are our hearts
being lifted from us toward the day.
Forty days passed at last.
Here now is an end
of waiting.

This is the day that the Lord has made.

I would like to say something of how quiet
was the hunt of the hawk against
the blue morning sky.

The field I stood against
was as black as that hawk. She circled
and our eyes met as she pulled away,
glad of the quiet and held upon the air.

SILVER CREEK

You pressed and shifted and steered it
and we got that old car up into the hills.
All the grass was green and the forest was wet.
All that grew was soft. The winter was over.
That had been the winter when we saw the hawk
from your window. Our coffee was warm
but it was not so black as that hawk
against that white winter sky.

We fixed our food by a waterfall while fog
fell in across the tops of the trees.
Beavers in the area laid low and we
said about the day, of this day
the joy of this good day.

We were the first in the forest since the thaw.
The path was mud. The falls was heavy
and fast, water from everywhere raced to it.
At the bottom, heads back,
we caught drops in our eyes and our eyes
turned flowers, some of the first since the thaw.

But never again then. Not again there.
The old buggy brought us home and the
sun rolled back the fog. Those beavers
will build a new dam this spring.
The end of a prayer. The end of a day together.
Always short.

I wish I could top those trees
like the birds do.

The road down into the orchard isn't
traveled by trucks anymore. It leans
down that steep side of the hill and
seeps in among the trees, a pathway
from a different kind of time.

Those were the days of monks and migrants
picking cherries with the deer, squeezing
peaches, and gathering apples in the
cool cellar days of the fall.

Each tree still holds sweet
yellow and red sacks, matching colors with
the autumn leaves landing like apples against
the tired dirt.

I know. I know. You had cut down
with me across that road. There were
trees hanging over so low that no
truck now could pass. We looked out
across the tops of those trees. Those birds.
And the valley beyond.

But when we passed through and walked along
past the apples, which of us knew if it
was 1957 again or not. In '57 I
was six and you were twenty. At the end
of a day, the sun could hold this orchard
like it holds it now. Colors would be the
same. Birds the same. The fruit hanging.

Which of us knew. Did you know.
Each tree still holds out cold apples.
Deer work the other end of the orchard.

When I see the moon, I always
remember something if
I am alone. I remember
the time when I saw the moon
and heard a locomotive miles
in the distance away.

I lived in the mountains
and there were six of us there
alone. It was black in the mountains
at dark. It was dark
and you could hear yourself walk.
It was black in the dark
and there was nothing to be afraid of:
it was where we lived.

There was a shed. There was nothing
in it and I never went in.
One night I was sitting by it.
The moon had come. I heard
the locomotive, it was miles away.
You could see the hills, the
moon had come. I heard
that thing, she whistled, miles away
she whistled and pulled.

I looked at those two dark hills
and saw them and heard
that train pulling and saw her,
saw her pulling. By the shed.
In the mountains where we lived.
Miles away.
Six of us alone.

Everywhere are buds when
the season of spring begins in March.

Near the place where the
early flowers will soon show,
two bugs
roll through the dirt
finally feeling new again.

Two hawks hunted all day on
the wind.
In the large sky
the warm air blew
and easily the hawks pulled up
on top of it.

It's over.
This poem and the winter
are over.

DUST

In the morning on the back side of
our house
the little pieces of them
I can see better in the morning
when the sun comes along.

I see
when the sun comes along
little pieces floating
and I would say
swarming

because

In the evening
in front of Mary Margaret's house
we used to say
swarming
for the mosquitoes
that could be seen
swarming
when in the evening
the sun came along.

When the sun comes along
all the sky
is blue
from the
swarming
of the dust.

POEM

The new green
shooting out of branches
on all these fir trees
is so soft
that it cannot
even hold
a small bird doing business,
a sparrow.

When fish are green
it will be the green
fir
of the new spring fir
on the Douglas fir tree
with its new green,
fishier by far
than the year old green
that will be the
green
when bears are green.

The whole sea and the mountain rivers
growl
and swim in the wind.

JEFF

Jeffrey is the tallest person that I know.
Jeffrey is so high that
when I hug him
I stand on a chair to.

At the top of it all
is his head of course
at the top of Jeffrey he has his head.

And when I look up there
when I'm looking for him
when I find him at his head
I smile and I say

Jeffrey you are the tallest person whom I know
and then I stand on the chair and hug him.

When June has grass the cats can hide
and lovers could hide too.
There are grasses so high in June
that lovers and cats could be
        hiding
        by May
and in June for sure so high
        grasses so high
        that
oh when the wind blows
thousands of skinny dancing ladies with their wrists
                                    toward the sky
sway sway and sway.

At a breezy time when the sun goes down
and the lake would be cool
the grasses by June
are more than only green
but like dancing women with feathered wrists
red wrists and purple
gray even
and brown.
Oh see the dancing millions at their fun
heaving pollen puffs of pollen down the hillsides
                                    toward the sun.

POEM

The butterfly
  passing the pansy

made me know
  that a pansy

is a butterfly
  on a stem.

The sun is low today, low in the sky and it is
as high as it could be. Thus it goes in winter
and in the fall. More so in the winter than in
the fall. More low. More very low. So it goes.
There it is as high as it shall go and not long
at all till dark. Three red sumacs. Then
later, in winter, it will be very more low.

The day splashed open
like a thousand birds bathing
but Grizzly Bear lies dreaming
of the day before, he
spent with me.

I had found him dancing
among the berries. We roared
together. He had beat
the earth for a drum and
it had sent the sun
high into the sky. Snorts
of light fell shafted
through the trees.
"Only today, only today,"
I heard the whole forest say.
And it was so. Then
the bear went away and
I was amazed that
we had met and
roared. I thought
all night of how we
had danced and slid
down together. I thought
all night. And look:
Grizzly Bear still lies dreaming
of the day before he
spent with me.

A thousand birds sing
for the fox
who walks
through the grass.

Elsewhere:
an Arab
changes feet quickly
in the hot sand.

I found Grizzly Bear dancing
among the berries. He
laughed when he
rolled over the hill.

O phrases from a morning,
join this phrase
of mine to your day:
give me a
dance
like the
Arab and the Bear.
Give me bugs
in the grass where
I'll walk.
Give me the fox for a friend.

THE MOTH

A moth
in the morning
I see flying
is so small
but
to me is small
not to himself

He beats his way by
and near
the top of the tall fir tree
which to me is tall
not to itself
something of a moth is beating
away at the morning
past the fir tree
and long out
over the valley

The moth
the little red moth
is a hero beating by
a high
red
(dressed up the sun shines on him)
hero beating by.

Taller trees still catch the light
while in the shorter ones,
day's light dies.

The air in the trees says
Good good
Good Night
leaning them
west
in a large, smooth
gesture of praise.

The final flashing
of birds
toward their nest.

The final banging
of a bee
toward the hive.

The still
moment
before
the singing sounds
of the night.

SNOW

Mt. Hood off its base is dancing a polka
while squirrels, like statues of the Buddha,
wait for the fox to pass.

It had grown light with the terrific sound of the wind.
Trees and the grasses stood up into the air.
There was again the morning and the day.

Snow like this was very early. Sun was
to be more expected. Still not even
all the nuts had been gathered and
the sun did come after the night of the storm.
Leaves, though late, had stayed
and there were all across the ground
colors and items that seldom
are there with snow.
The red leaves and the still, very green grass.
It was brilliant by the sun and
then clouds came sneezing over the mountains
making a grayer blue than the sky.

One time, two times, three times this winter
may there be a wild walk like this
for me and that fox.

I was walking on a hill against a strong wind
and there suddenly realized
that it was the wind itself
that was making this happen

the wind hit my body and bowed it
                    like a sail
and pushed a boat load of sentences through me

but on top of them all
were left a few bright and breezy words,

the poem.

HOUSE

House.
House with a jug
on the porch

with leaves
overshadowing
the chimney

with a door
and with
the windows

and then House where a sweet lady appears
in passing a window and disappears

and from where smoke
rises, from the House
where she tells
the children a story

far larger than
the world

in her House
far larger than
the world.

EACH DAY

Dawn—with tremendous courtesy—
begins to break the darkness all apart.

Roosters scream the desperate plight
of the conquered night,

which night is surely, if slowly,
undone

not accused by the light
nor abused by its might

simply removed by the light

Slowly, courteously, totally.
Each day.

The trumpet man
and the cello lady
are ready to blow
and pull whatever sounds
the conductor says

And the flute man and the violin lady
wait for the sign that will let them join.

Oh wondrous and careful obedience,
joyful readiness for saving sounds

When his hand says,
then sound out for all of us
a good sweet beat,
and a true pure sound

pull the notes that will stir the sea within
find the chords that make the planets spin
blend the sighs of the gracefully dying
with rhythms from the upper air

Watch your conducting man
watch his hand,
for he was there when the mountains were made
and he knew the time when still color had sound

The hand that moves your music
is the hand that moves the stars.

Across
water like glass
a fast
and sudden
wind
races.

In two directions almost the same:
a flash of ripples.

An angel slicing
     the waters
     of
     the pond,
delivering a message
to the bottom.

Fast again to heaven returned,
the waters all smooth,

the earth blessed.

KITE

Frail household going up over the sea,
    I follow you.

This string is my body unwinding
    and able to go high.

The wind and a little house made of paper
    take me.

We have the sky when
    I cut the string:

Ah, we are forever out over the sea,
we are forever upward.

Days of flying have tired them—
kite and string.

Three windy days past
they were let go
    over the sea

the last catchers of sunset light
the first seers of new turned day
the only fliers in the night's
    salty sky.

Now—weakened by adventure—
kite splinters in the sky

and string lays herself weakly
and meekly down
across nine hundred feet of the sea.

CARNIVAL

At carnival—a girl
dressed as a tomato:
Mary the Tomato
strode the lawn

and the boys,
all wild at her red,
came running behind
and clowns in the swings screamed,
wild as well
about this walking dish, and

Three dragons gathered too
joined by a radished child
when Mary the Tomato
sang her song

I am a tomato
I am I
You are tomatoes
and we can fly

I am a red one
and I am round
You are red ones
and we grow in the ground . . .

Crazy went the song
and crazy went the throng:

Monsters and tulips danced
Tigers and maidens pranced
Cowboys and professors raced
while mocking birds
    in getups
    gave chase.

Oh that was a gay and twirling march
of creatures and critters and types,
all friends and made fair,
each lovely and all kind,
feet abeat upon the ground
all moving now and forward,
the laughing and the song
the flashing of wings and swords
forward and across the ground

and at the head
could be seen the red, red
tomato
still striding and
round and bright as ever
lovely too and laughing:

I am I
You are
and we can.

Mary the Tomato led them all.

THE KID AS CLOWN

Collin, when four,
was a clown
    with his mother

and the two of them
could throw oranges
    in great circles

always catch them
and quickly throw them
    again.

He threw with a face white
like a daisy's
and his lips were as red
as a race.
His gown was a zebra
gone green and

He would enter as a bird:
arms up high
head cocked back
only three toes
    left on the ground.

A great voice in the sky announced him:
"The Kid Collin As a Clown!"

Mine is the view a bird might have,

for I am on a hill
    and the wind hits me good.
    Its blowing holds me high.

    I stay here taking the valley
    with my eyes and see
    other birds below me. I see

    people have cut the wheat. Its
    golden stubble could make a glo-
    rious home for me.
    Its entire color

bounces through me and I feel the roll of the land.

I go higher. I want to go up beyond (all) stars.
I will take the golden color with me.
I will take the memory of the rolling land.

AUGUST PRAYER

The monks chant their prayer in the hot church
but their heart is not in it.
Only their vows bring them and keep them
at the hot and useless task.

Gone are the sweet first good days
when prayer and singing came easy
Gone as well many brothers
who used to stand here singing
    the feasts with them.

They know there are ways to beat this heat
and that Americans everywhere are finding them
but they beat instead the tones of psalms
    and, *by beating,*
      fall through the layers of heat
      and the layers of prayer

    and are standing there now
    only with their sound
    and their sweat

everything taken from them
except the way that this day in August has been.

A long dry pine needle
slips between your foot and your sandal.

You take it for awhile and then
you bend down to take it out.

Your companions continue on
and though you see them and hear them still,

you are alone for a mighty moment
in a great flash of peace.

EVENING SONG

The mountain man made hay all day
with the luck of the autumn sun,

and as night falls—*his daughters already asleep,*
his wife awaiting him at the door—
he sings this prayer from the steep hillside:

Holy this ground.
Holy this mountain.
Holy the air in a circle around it.

Ring of Gold from the starry sky,
come settling down in a circle around us
and make

Holy the mountain
Holy the night.

The world on the verge of its last evening—

when suddenly, breaking out from the womb
of a most pure virgin,
comes running the Word,
            the Bridegroom!

            (as if out from some bridal chamber)

and courses like the Sun through the sky,

            A Champion and
            Day bursting out
            from the verge of night.

(Inspired by a tenth century Latin Vespers hymn:
Vergente mundi vespere
Uti sponsus de thalamo
Egressus honestissima
Virginis matris clausula.)

FOGGY WALK

Soft, soft, soft the fog on our faces
in early winter's early afternoon.
And we are walking in the world
as a hushed and silent watery womb,

> *Twins or something!*
> coming round
> a first time to consciousness,
> whispering the wonder of it all

> > *What was that!*
> > *Birds! Oh.*
> > *Only for a moment and*
> > *then gone*
> > *in the fog*
> > *and wet like us.*

We seem not afraid—foolishly perhaps—
to be coming out soon
into the light

to see and touch all the rest
and to be seen and touched by them.

When they see that you are beautiful,
will they know that
we have walked together in here?

The earth asleep a season
and birdsong few

the gliding clouds
and the immense quiet

soggy soil yet
already the noiseless
push of the green.

This afternoon the light
was clearly longer than
 yesterday
 and the day
 before.

Let us celebrate the light
 tonight.
let us light a candle
 and a tree.

Far stars shall see
our hopeful signals
and let down mercies
 and *skyly* strengths

waking the earth
stirring the birds
drying the soil
and pulling the green.

In the icy blue light
of the January afternoon
 smoke
 rises
 straight up
from the cabin in the
distant hills,

a strip of prayers
in the blue distance.

Nothing moves except
the silent sun, taking
its early winter dive

 and
with this poem, I
dive with the sun
and rise with the smoke
and crush this cold
stillness into a prayer
for whoever is there
in the hills making smoke

and say
Go, prayer, into the sky,
go slowly up with

the smoke
and bring back the sun
from its early dive

for the warmer and longer days,
the buzzing busy
time of the spring.

DYING
(for Amah)

This long
and final
breathing
tries
to touch
so low
    inside
that she finally
dies,

alive at last to whom
this final breathing tries to touch.

SAYING GOOD-BYE

Last evening
the sky was gold
at sunset where
there was a
crack in the clouds

and when the plane
you were on
roared up into the
sky behind me

my whole body pulled skyward
after you but
not nearly
fast enough
to ever catch a
glimpse of you again
today or to
touch you from behind,
barely.

Instead, I was pulled
earthward as well
and cracked like the clouds
as the great gold
sun of the air

came between my
earthly and skyward parts
and burned light
forever into me,

light forever
from the split
of your going away.

And you and I go up toward the moon

So still the night
So graced
So utterly bathed in light
Utterly pure, good night.

And you so far away from me!
How good it would be
     to look on you
     and see your shining eyes
     loving me.

But mountains and plains and even an ocean
stand between such (oh, I need it) looking

and so then

You and I are up toward the moon—
Mistress!
Point of reference high enough
     in the sky
     to hang our looking on.

You I see. You I touch.
You it is who bathe me
in utterly pure
     good light.

Last year
      under this same August moon,
I wrote a poem for you from here
and stretched with it all the way across the sea
to where you were waiting to hear from me.

This year
      the moon herself is writing the poem
with smooth, easy streams of light
that wash all across this page
and make it say:

> *Hey, a happy summer*
> *Hey, the breezy night*
> *Hush—a sky for lovers*
> *Hey, the night is bright.*

And I know this moon is holding you
      —round and far and good—
And how she holds,
that's how I hold;
how she calls,
that's how I call,
I say:

> *"Coming down on you now,*
> *Coming down with light for you,*
> *Coming down all around you,*
> *Here for you tonight."*

DARK WOOD

Tree tops and scattered clouds
hid the full and rising moon from me,
but the breezy night pushed well,
and swaying trees gave light a chance

so that I knew there was a moon around
and if I waited
    this whole night could become white.

I lay there in the cool and rustling grass
and let the wind move over me.
    I did not move,
      but the clouds did
      and above me the branches danced hard.

This whole dark wood came aglow;
it became a vision of my soul,
for I lay there thinking of you, and

    You—you are light
    climbing in my soul
    setting loose all its wooden branches
    for a soft and fluid swaying in the air

And now with you
all my dark wood is moving and dancing
and above me is a great opening to the sky
where light climbs in
and plants a face:

You, the full and rising moon.

TALKING ONE NIGHT

We talked pretty late into the night.
There was so much to say.
I just had to give you some of what I'd had
from the moon last month

and now there she was again
rolling low through the sky
    waxing
       falling lower while we talked.

Soon you'd be gone, I knew,
but when you were home again
she'd be full and high in the sky
           and I thought maybe you'd see
           what I'd seen.

I'd seen

    Each face I ever loved,
    Each face forming one fine face,
    This face becoming the Ruler's face,
    and then the Ruler's face flying and
    touching everything soft with light.

The Ruler sending the night's good wind
while helping creatures crawl
and sharpening ridges on the mountains.
And then the Ruler's face kissing each lake
and found in every pond.
Him pulling the oceans hard,
him visiting plants through the night
and then him even guiding geese in flight.

The Ruler was each one I ever loved,
He took the faces of them all.
And I just had to tell you
because I knew when I saw you
  —a new acquaintance
   a new friend—
I knew that this month would be different some

and that I'd see your face when the Ruler climbed high.
I'd see him taking *you* into Night's wondrous sky.

This line is for love.
          And this line also for love.
These all are lines layed down
     by love.

And I am laying them down
as carefully, as sweetly, as strongly
as ever I lay you down.
You and these lines, I am laying down

and between these lines and you
I also lay down my *yes*
to the thousand miles between us

     and *yes*
     in a line layed down

reaches across the stinging distance,
reaches and touches your wide eyes
and then closes them, whispering,

"*Yes*. I love you."

An   iris   is
     iris-   is-   (t) able

even   for   ire,

     for even for the Iris-h ire
     an   iris   is   irenic
     in the extreme.

THE NIGHT OF ST. JOHN
(June 23 to June 24)

If, from the moon,
(or even higher—say,
from another planet or some near star)
You could somehow gaze well as far as Earth
and watch her tilted and rolling,
you would see at this hour a longer strip of Light
    than any other time around.

But come down now,
    much, much further down
and move along the edge
where the Day turns to Night.

Do you see a little city in the mountains,
and do you see their watch fires glow?
Slip in under the twilight split,
come all the way down now
and move along easy with the people
    toward the Square.

The lady jumps beautifully.
Jumps clean.
Jumps clear.
Cuts a circle with her curves.
And these mountains—rising, falling—
They are her rhythm and her song.

In her legs are the bending skies.
In her stretching back is a planet
    with light stretching away.
In her reaching fingers I see the promise
    of a night filled with stars.

Anything at all can happen tonight . . . and will.
For this dancing helps to bend the sky wide open,
and the power of all the stars
will pour into our unseeing flesh
    and make it fresh again.

Then's when I'll stand up like a Lion
and take you in my arms
and we will spin a midsummer night's dance
that drills all the way through to the other side
    of the galaxy.

We will roar so loud about
the Grace of this night
that every demon that blocks our loving well
will be chased away again to his icy home
and stay there stuck.
Then only joy and power will be left for us.

And tomorrow at the river
we'll dip ourselves in Salvation
and then lay ourselves down
in Summer's perfect Sun
singing,

Glory. Power. Wisdom. And Strength.
Praise to the Bridegroom.
All the Earth is his.

Ages and ages of moons hitting these mountains.
Snows shining through millions of nights.
The human time here—one thousand years,
or at the most maybe two.
And yet of these years,
I am here this one night,
and the moon and the mountains
        seem mine.

A wise warm wind rushes night now through these valleys.
It makes me think:
    I can put a prayer on the wind
    and send it up over the long hills,
And so I say,

            Snows, wonder with me about the
            Maker of moon and mountains and my wide eyes.
            Turn with me—spin with me!—
            this one night more around,
            and let me pass with you on the pointed peaks
            this turn, this time being hit by moon and stars.

The prayer goes. The prayer is sent.
And then   Wait, Wind, I say,
take this one more word up high:

            Snows, say with me:
            Maker, make me white.
            Maker, make me pure.
            Maker, make me light.

EPIGRAPH
MONK'S CELL

Ten-
der-
ness

while I rest.

And all goodly hope
beside me.